The Independent Learner

A Guide to Creative
Independent Study

Teacher's Manual

Starr Cline

AN AUTHORS GUILD BACKINPRINT.COM EDITION

The Independent Learner
A Guide to Creative Independent Study

AN AUTHORS GUILD BACKINPRINT.COM EDITION

Published by iUniverse, Inc.

For information address:
iUniverse, Inc.
1663 Liberty Drive
Bloomington, IN 47403
www.iuniverse.com

Because of the dynamic nature of the Internet, any Web addresses
or links contained in this book may have changed
since publication and may no longer be valid.

The views expressed in this work are solely those of the author and do not necessarily
reflect the views of the publisher, and the publisher hereby disclaims any responsibility
for them.

ISBN: 978-0-595-49120-9

Printed in the United States of America

Dedicated to:

> Jerry
> Adam
> Larry

Special thanks to friend and advisor, Dr. A. H. Passow, Teachers College, Columbia University.

With sincere appreciation I would like to acknowledge the teachers who assisted in field testing the manual:

> Suzanne Bauer
> Susan Bernstein
> Betty Bogart
> Danny Domingo
> Harriet Finkelstein
> Jim Fredericks
> Ann Todes and especially
> Cheryl Caplin - my co-teacher

I would also like to acknowledge the support given to me by the Herricks School District, New Hyde Park, New York:

> Dr. Leon R. Pierce, Superintendent
> Dr. Ronald M. Barnes, Ass't. Superintendent for Instruction
> Mr. John H. Bauer, Ass't. Superintendent for Business
> Mrs. Patricia Galaskas, Administrative Assistant
> Dr. Charlotte Podolsky, Director of Special Education
> Dr. John Crowley, Principal, Center Street School
> Mr. Eugene Goldwasser, Principal, Denton Avenue School
> Mrs. Nancy Lindenauer, Principal, Searingtown School

Contents

Section

Preface 6

Foreword 8

I. Goals of the Manual 9
    Why Independent Study 9
    Definition of Independent Study 10
    Goals of Independent Study for the Gifted Child 11

II. The Gifted Child 13
    General Characteristics and Identification of the Gifted 13
    Social and Emotional Characteristics 15

III. The Teacher's Role in Independent Study 18
    The Role of the Teacher 18
    Student's Goals 18
    Teacher's Goals 19

IV. The Independent Study Begins 21
    Getting Students Started 21
    Selecting a Topic for Study 22
    Differentiating the Curriculum for the Gifted 22
    Project or Product Development 29
    Summary 30

V. Troubleshooting Some Common Problems 31
    Getting Students Started 31
    Topic Selection Problems 31
    Project Anxiety 34
    Student is Difficult to Motivate 34
    Student Appears to Have Low Self-Esteem 35
    Student has Difficulty Accepting Criticism 35

VI. Typical Independent Studies Done By Students 36
    Sample Topics Chosen by Students 36
    Examples of Studies Done by Students 37

VII. Developing Resources 40

    Developing Outside Resources for Independent Study 40

    People 40

    Community Resources 41

    Local Agencies or Groups 42

    Special Written or Audio-Visual Materials 42

    Resource Bibliography 43

VIII. Independent Study Program Management 47

    Developing Independent Study as a Curricular Option 47

IX. Evaluation of Independent Study 50

    Selecting Procedures 50

    Sample Evaluation Forms 52

X. Appendix 64

    1. Student Interest Inventory 65

    2. Student Information from Parents 67

    3. Resource Development Questionnaire 69

    4. Creative Problem Solving 70

Bibliography 82

Student Resource Book 84

Preface

Independent study, as a learning strategy, has been used primarily at the secondary, college and university levels. It has also been used with gifted children. This guide can be used by teachers in heterogeneous settings or in homogeneous classes and also in pullout programs for gifted students. The guide discusses the role of the teacher working with students involved in independent study. It stresses curriculum differentiation for the gifted. It also assists the teacher in identifying and planning for gifted students. The guide identifies possible problems which might arise and offers suggestions for dealing with them. The guide also includes evaluation of independent study, program management, and development of resources.

A Resource Book for students is available as a companion to the teacher's manual for students to use as a guide when working independently.

Independent study, properly, guided can make a significant contribution toward the development of an independent creative learner - the goal of education.

Frank Williams developed a three dimensional model expressing the education process in terms of student behaviors, teacher behaviors and the delivery of content in the various disciplines.

A Model for Implementing Cognitive-Affective
Behaviors in the Classroom

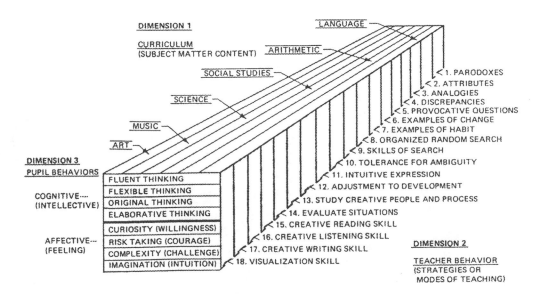

The effective teacher understands the characteristics of the student in order to assist him/her toward becoming an independent, creative learner.

Sylvia Rimm, Joanne Rand Whitmore, Rita and Kenneth Dunn, Anthony Gregor, Frank Williams and Theodore Callisto identify the following learner characteristics: intellectual ability, creative ability, motivation, interests, needs and learning styles as significant factors for the teacher to know about his/her student in order to be effective.

The process skills of the student will be developed by the types of processes provided and encouraged in the learning environment; skills such as creative thinking, critical thinking, problem-solving, research and inquiry.

These process skills need to be interfaced with content competencies such as exploration, specific inquiry methods and advanced enrichment topics.

Keeping all these in proper balance is a responsibility shared by the active learner and the facilitating teacher.

Good classroom management skills greatly assist this process. The teacher needs a well defined set of guidelines for record keeping, evaluation procedures, product completion, and vehicles for students to share with audiences. Most of all, the teacher sets the tone for an environment where it is okay to risk, to think "out loud" - a thinking/learning/caring/sharing place. Process and environment are the key elements.

Joanne Rand Whitmore (Giftedness, Conflict and Underachievement) points out that the two most important factors affecting a student's progress toward successful classroom behavior as an independent learner are self-image and the learning environment itself.

A person arrives at a self image (good or bad) based on perceptions of self which are received from those in his/her environments - home, neighborhood and, in large measure, at school. (Callisto, Theodore A.; Slosson, Steven W.; Observational Analysis)

In a school setting, learning will be enhanced or hindered by the student's self image (based on perception) in terms of "I can learn" or "I cannot learn." One gets feedback or perceptions of self primarily from teachers and the learning processes that either help or hinder his/her learning. The interface between and among learning processes, learning styles and content competencies will affect how, what and whether one learns.

Independent study is an excellent vehicle that can pull together all of the positive elements leading toward an independent, creative learner.

This teacher guide and the student resource book are designed to assist the teacher and the student toward that goal.

Foreword

The goal of developing an independent learner is one of the more important goals of education. It is a goal which figures prominently in the literature on gifted education but it is one which we should set for all children. Independent study--a term that actually encompasses a variety of educational practices--is widely advocated as a means for developing independent learners. Unfortunately, many teachers have not reflected on the process and seem to believe that if they simply tell their students "to study independently" that is sufficient. For some, if students are working by themselves on the same assignment, that is considered independent study. And, in fact, there is a concept of independent study which is basically an audiotutorial method--the learner interacting with some instructional material on an individual basis. However, Starr Cline's concept of independent study is different. She views independent study as a process by which learners acquire the skills and attitudes which enable them to function independently, becoming "independent learners."

The two manuals--one for teachers and one for students--are aimed at helping both understand the concept of independent study as a means of developing independent learners and at providing the insights for implementing that concept. While Dr. Cline focuses on independent study for students with special gifts and talents, the process and techniques she presents are equally important for all learners, as she points out. These are documents which are intended to be conceptual--i.e., to communicate the conceptual base for independent study--and practical--i.e., to assist teachers and students to engage in independent study and to "do it better." I think readers will find them helpful, especially if they read the guides as discussions of ideas and not as cook books full of recipes.

A. Harry Passow
Jacob H. Schiff Professor of Education
Teachers College, Columbia University

I

Goals of the Manual

Why Independent Study

Mere interest or ambition is not nearly sufficient to allow one entrance to the elite independent study group at my school. One must have a certain IQ score (this, to me, is an ambiguous system), a certain grade point average (what of genius under-achievement), and satisfactory teacher recommendations. That last one is a killer, too. I do not feel one's personality should be judged to win a few hours of time to learn if one craves them.

A better way, it seems to me, would be to have a panel of advisors who could interview interested students about their own independent program proposals and, after judging their ideas and capabilities, decide which ones could handle the independent situation. The other way around, you have to beat the standard system -- which turns some kids into zombies -- before you can exercise any initiative of your own. Sometimes that's all we need to make life (and learning) interesting in the required classes.

An independent study program is definitely an asset, since it allows freedom to work on what you want and at what speed you wish. For instance, I am currently monitoring the pollution levels of local streams and rivers. This is especially gratifying because the data actually does some good. This is the reward for often boring work. The results are given to the conservation commission of our town where they are reviewed and published. Something is accomplished and, whether they know it or not, people are benefiting. Working for a high grade is not nearly as exciting as seeing your work help others. It's really a great personal life. (Krueger, 1978, pp. 74-75.)

Every teacher is a teacher of the gifted child. There are gifted children in every classroom. Some students are generally precocious, and excel in all areas, and others possess talents and abilities in special areas. All teachers have a responsibility to their students to identify talents and abilities and plan for them.

This manual has been written with the following goals in mind:

1. To assist the classroom teacher in identifying students with special gifts and talents.

2. To assist teachers of the gifted in identifying areas of giftedness at an early age.

3. To assist teachers in appropriately differentiating the independent study curriculum for the gifted.

4. To provide a guide to independent study for students, which will help them to become self-directed learners.

Definition of Independent Study

Independent study can be defined as "the student's self-directed pursuit of academic competence in as autonomous manner as he is able to exercise at any particular time" (Dressel & Thompson, 1973, p. 1). The independent study is a process which includes the following steps:

1. Student selects the topic to be studied.

2. Teacher guides the student as the student designs the study and formulates key questions.

3. Student learns the appropriate research skills and/or basic skills and expanded basic skills relevant to the topic.

4. Teacher reviews the student's basic outline for the study and makes suggestions so that educational ideas which differentiate the curriculum are included.

5. Student and teacher locate appropriate resources for the study.

6. Student conducts necessary research.

7. Student is responsible for broadening or narrowing topic. Teacher assists when necessary.

8. Student is allowed as much time as is deemed necessary to conduct the research.

9.   If the student becomes aware of problems associated with the study, problem solving strategies are taught which assist in seeking solutions.

10.   Student is responsible for designing way in which he/she communicates what has been learned. Various kinds of media are used. The student chooses the way in which material will be presented, i.e., authors a book, produces a slide-sound program, video show, makes a film strip, presents a chalk talk, etc.

11.   Student evaluates what has been accomplished in terms of individual capabilities and assesses independent study as an appropriate learning strategy, helping the students to become educational connoisseurs.

12.   Teacher assists in seeking appropriate audiences for completed projects, i.e., classmates, peers, parents, professional publications, contests, etc.

Goals of Independent Study for the Gifted Child

As a society we must view talents and abilities as a natural resource which deserves to be nurtured and developed. With the proper training and guidance the gifted child can acquire a knowledge base, apply what he has learned, analyze and begin to synthesize information. Hopefully this will help him/her to become a producer of information. Early identification of aptitudes is important, in the development of special abilities. If we look to musicians and athletes who achieved recognition for outstanding achievements in their fields (Pressey, 1955), we note certain patterns emerging. Those who achieved eminence had excellent opportunities for the ability to develop as well as encouragement from family and friends.

1.   Superior and early continuing individual guidance instruction was present.

2.   They had opportunities to frequently and continually practice and extend their capability and to progress as they were able.

3.   There was a close association with others in the field which generally fostered the abilities of all concerned.

4.   They had strong success experiences which were acclaimed.

At any age, development of any ability is fostered by a favorable immediate environment, expert instruction, frequent progressive opportunities to exercise the ability, social facilitation, and frequent success experiences.

Independent study allows intellectual talents and abilities to be nurtured in this same way. Similar experiences can be provided.

11

Specific goals of independent study for the gifted child are listed below:

1. To have gifts and talents identified.

2. Once potential areas of giftedness are identified, basic and expanded basic skills in areas of interest will be acquired. Talents and abilities will be nurtured and developed in preparation for a satisfying life style.

3. To learn research skills which enable the student to become an independent self-directed learner.

4. To become aware that knowledge is worth having and that knowledge is worthy of pursuit.

5. To become educational connoisseurs.

6. To gain self-esteem by having energies positively directed.

7. To be exposed to materials which allow the use of higher level thought processes.

8. To appreciate and accept one's own talents and abilities.

9. To be prepared to become producers of information in the future.

In many cases gifted children have varied interests which extend beyond regular curriculum areas and beyond those of their peers. They often feel different and do not always view their differences in a positive manner. According to Ross and Parker (1980), "in contrast to their positive academic self-concepts, gifted youngsters seem to possess relatively poorer social self-concepts" (p. 7). Some begin to hide their ideas as well as their feelings so that they might be more acceptable to their age mates when working with students with independent study. Teachers may bring them in touch with intellectual peers rather than age mates, as well as mentors and professionals in the field. This helps avoid the possibility that the gifted child will grow up feeling alone or left out.

Students who complete independent study projects sometimes become "experts" in particular subject areas. They can be called upon to share their expertise with appropriate audiences. This helps them to develop leadership skills and bolsters their self-esteem.

As students design a product which communicates what they have learned, additional talents may be discovered and creative abilities encouraged. When independent study is an option, some children's interests are allowed to come to the fore at an early age.

Research skills can be taught in areas of interest. Students can be intellectually stimulated and guided into using higher level thought processes. Research skills should be considered to be a part of the basic skills curriculum for the gifted. Learning how to find information, how to refine it and how to communicate it is essential to becoming a producer of information. Providing the gifted child with these skills frees him to learn on his own in the hope that he will become a life-long learner and lover of knowledge.

II

The Gifted Child

General Characteristics and Identification of the Gifted

Some measures commonly used by schools to identify their gifted students include the following:

I.Q.

Teacher Nomination

Parent Identification

Self Nomination

Creativity Tests

The curriculum can serve as an additional method for identifying giftedness. Passow (1981), referring to work done with Tannenbaum (Passow & Tannenbaum. 1981), suggests that rather than viewing identification and educational differentiation as a two step diagnostic prescriptive model, that prescribed enrichment (such as independent study) can become a vehicle for identification. This can be used to facilitate enrichment. As a student selects a particular topic for study, the teacher can ascertain skills necessary to that area of study and design an educational plan for the student. For example, students selecting a topic in the area of science would be introduced to the investigative tools used by scientists. They would learn how to formulate hypotheses and design and record experiments. Expanded basic skills would be taught when necessary. Expanded topic skills refer to skills necessary to performance of tasks related to careers. These skills might not be a part of the curriculum at that particular time. Students choosing chemistry would learn about the metric system and the periodic table well before it was available as a part of the curriculum. Students exhibiting a talent for writing poetry would be exposed to complex forms of meter and rhyme at an earlier age than would normally be prescribed. The child's talents and abilities have dictated the direction of instruction. Instruction allows a student to perform in a more sophisticated manner. As he/she progresses, instruction is redesigned to meet new needs. Given the required skills, capable students will perform in a way and exhibit behaviors which society considers gifted.

Following are some of characteristics or behaviors of the gifted child (Isaacs, 1971; Terman & Oden, 1947; Treffinger, 1975), many of which can be noted as students work on independent study:

1. Curious, asks many questions

2. Long term memory

3. Persistent

4. Independent

5. Able to sustain interest in more than one field

6. Learns easily

7. Creative and imaginative

8. Self-sufficient

9. Original

10. Sets high goals

11. Has special talents

12. Uses scientific research method

13. Sees relationships and draws generalities

14. Creates new ideas

15. Initiates own activities

16. Exhibits leadership

17. Likes to invent and build mechanical devices

18. Applies learning from one situation to another

19. Continually questions the status quo

Children exhibiting six or more characteristics may be gifted (Isaacs, 1971).

Independent study can serve more than one purpose. As children are given the opportunity to become involved in a study, teachers can look for and observe student behaviors. Teachers can begin to identify specific talents and can design an educational plan based on these observations.

Social and Emotional Characteristics

If one is to meet his/her potential, social and emotional needs must be met, as well as intellectual ones. As educators, it is our responsibility to consider the whole child as we design an educational plan. As Roeper (1982) puts it:

It is my belief that concern for the emotional development of the gifted should become part of the educational process. I am hoping more research will be done in this area and that parents, social workers, psychologists, administrators and teachers will become interested in this aspect of the gifted child. (p. 24)

The gifted have very special needs and must be given special support to aid them in their development.

Terrassier (1979) describes the gifted child in relation to the syndrome of dyssynchrony. There exists a discrepancy between the rapidity of their mental development and the average development which is recognized and taught in the school. Dyssynchrony also appears in the relationships they establish with other children. Intellectual mates are frequently older. A student involved in an independent study can be intellectually stimulated and introduced to others with similar interests regardless of age. Terrassier (1979) also states that there is usually dyssychrony between psychomotor and intellectual development. Teachers often expect the gifted child to perform at higher levels in all areas, but this is not always possible. Difficulties in handwriting, especially in boys, are quite common. Children are often frustrated by their inability to have their hands function as quickly as their minds. Teachers working with these students can encourage them to find creative ways for communicating information which might not involve writing. In some cases psychomotor and affective development may not be on the same level as their intellectual development. Parents and educators sometimes have difficulty accepting such dyssynchronic behaviors. The school system asks the child to progress in a homogrnous manner (Terrassier, 1979). Independent study can help to modify a student's program.

According to Altman (1983) and Roeper (1982) gifted children sometimes impose unrealistic standards on themselves. They sometimes become perfectionists and suffer from constant frustration, guilt and self-debasement. This sometimes comes through as they work on their studdies. Teachers can step in and point out the positive aspects of their work, helping them to become more realistic. Gifted students often have lower social self-concepts than their academic ones (Ross & Parker, 1980). They sometimes see others as being responsible for their achievements (Dirkes, 1983). In private conferences with students, teachers can help them to see and appreciate their efforts and abilities. Self-evaluation can help increase self-esteem and assist them in developing confidence. Students have reported this in conferences with the author.

15

They may prefer to immerse themselves in areas of primary interest but often feel pressured by adults to achieve excellence in all areas. Independent study can allow them to pursue their interests. Individual conferences with students and parents can help both to establish realistic goals for them so that parents and students can appreciate talents and abilities.

Many gifted students are well integrated but often become aware of the world's problems. This sometimes becomes apparent when a student touches sensitive problems or issues in his/her study, i.e., endangered species, world hunger, or crime and punishment. They feel compelled to stand up for their convictions while suffering loneliness and isolation for taking such risks. These children need the support of both family and teachers to help them to cope--not with their actions--but with the resulting feelings created by their reaction to their environment. In general, gifted students possess greater sensitivities to their total environment and they pick up non-verbal cues in their surroundings. They need to be encouraged to communicate their ideas and feelings. If they do not get the support and encouragement to be what they are and feel good about it, the danger exists that they will become bored or hide their gifts.

All children are special and many have "gifted parts". If teachers establish an atmosphere in their classrooms where specialness is permitted to emerge, where it is nurtured and developed and rewarded, both students and teachers will benefit.

Dirkes (1983, p. 70) produced a list of rights that children must have if they are to develop and fully utilize their giftedness. Among these are the right to contribute to one's own education and that of others; to be free to apply knowledge and creativity to new situations; to be different, have opinions and be respected.

It is the writer's contention that these rights constitute goals of independent study.

Whitmore (1980) discusses the minimal conditions for meeting the basic needs of the gifted which should be considered for independent study.

1. The student should have the opportunity to actively participate in planning and evaluating curriculum.

2. The teacher should serve as a model of a creative, intelligent, sensitive person who is socially skillful and who is actively involved in facilitating continuous learning and self-development.

3. Competition and cooperation should be appropriately balanced.

4. Students should be assisted in learning to cope with traits of perfectionism and supersensitivity.

5. Teachers should assist students in establishing realistic expectations for themselves.

6. A flexible schedule should be provided with minimal pressure.

7. The students should experience a sense of success in a challenging intellectual environment.

8. The students should experience a general sense of acceptance and belonging and should be in touch with other gifted peers and mentors with whom there can be frequent social and academic interaction.

9. The climate should communicate a feeling of genuine respect and affirmation of the worth of individuals.

10. There should be honest constructive feedback. Possibilities for the development of social skills and leadership potential should be explored.

11. Open communication should exist where the student can discuss ideas and raise questions without fear of ridicule.

12. The curriculum should be appropriately differentiated and individu- alized to meet the individual needs of each child involved in a study.

This manual is being written as one alternative which can be used to assist teachers in identifying gifts and designing or modifying existing curriculum which will meet the needs of these special students.

III.

The Teacher's Role in Independent Study

The Role of the Teacher

As the teacher begins assisting the student to design an independent study project both student and teacher must decide what goals and objectives each has that might be accomplished through the study. Following are goals students might select which can be addressed through independent study. Goals should include both cognitive and affective areas.

Students' Goals

1. Learn steps of independent study

2. Learn research skills

3. Extend resources outside of the classroom

4. Organize work

5. See more solutions to one problem

6. Generate more creative ideas in my work

7. Become more of a productive thinker

8. Feel better about myself

9. Find other people with my interests

10. Acquire knowledge of _____

11. Become more of a leader

12. Become an independent learner

13. Accept responsibility for work

14. Learn to take more chances, experiment and use ideas

15. Become more aware of strengths and weaknesses

16. Learn to work alone

17. Learn to make decisions

18. Learn to judge the usefulness of facts

19. Speak in front of small groups

20. Make a large group presentation

As students select their goals to work on, the teacher will begin to see how individual students view themselves. Private conferences discussing the goals might be helpful. Some students will select one or two. Some check ALL. This is usually an indication that these students are perfectionists and set unrealistic expectations for themselves.

Teachers' Goals

Teachers should establish their own set of goals for their students as well, which can be accomplished through independent study. Some suggestions follow:

1. To assist students in becoming self-directed learners.

2. To assist them in extending their resources.

3. To provide opportunities for them to work through curriculum that is differentiated.

4. To help them to become productive thinkers.

5. To provide support and encouragement which might help to increase the self-esteem of students.

6. To help them find appropriate audiences for their work.

7. To find intellectual peers for them.

8. To teach research skills.

After students and teachers have identified their goals, the teacher must establish priorities with the students. Because of the role we expect gifted children to play in society in the future, we must prepare them to become self-directed learners. The teacher must relinquish a command approach to teaching and move on to a discovery approach to learning on the part of the student. The teacher works with the students as they select what it is they wish to study. General goals and objectives for self-directed learning, developed by Treffinger (1975), are listed below. As teachers become aware of the steps involved, they can monitor their own behaviors.

Going from a command to a discovery approach may take time and involve steps along the way for both teacher and student. In a teacher directed or command mode the teacher decides, and prescribes for the entire class, |the content to be taught, the way it will be taught, resources which will be used and how it will be evaluated. In a self-directed or discovery mode the learner assumes total control of designing the educational program and develops his/her program, including evaluation procedures.

Interim steps would probably be required for both the teacher and student. Students may be given some control and provided with options at first in one small area. Teachers might then work collaboratively with students and design a program together. The teacher would then allow the student to design his/her program. As the teacher monitors the student's ability to assume responsibility for his/her learning, the teacher begins to assume the role of guide or facilitator. The teacher must be supportive and reassuring inasmuch as the student might not be comfortable at first. As a student is able to assume more control and responsibility, the teacher can then give the reigns to the student.

Both teacher and student may feel somewhat uncomfortable in their new roles. The transition for the teacher may take time and concentrated effort. The student may also need a great deal of support and encouragement. Taking responsibility for one's learning and making decisions may not come easily. Children need to become aware that there is no need to fear failure when learning how to learn. There are no "mistakes" but rather experiences that can be used to build upon.

Teachers should serve as role models for their students. They should share their own interests, hobbies and passions with their students. They should try to set aside time when students are able to talk about their interests and their concerns. Gifted students need adult communication and interaction. Teachers, however, should not feel that they need to be the source of all information for their students. As Renzulli (1982) put it:

> Teachers of the gifted cannot possibly be (or become) subject matter experts in the many topic areas in which their students are and should develop high levels of interest and this takes commitment. This is especially true at the elementary level where teachers are usually expected to provide services encompassing a variety of areas. (p. 154)

They should feel free to call upon experts at all levels and at all times. Gifted youngsters may have expertise in areas which exceeds that of the teacher. They need to be appreciated and respected for it.

IV

The Independent Study Begins

Getting Students Started

This manual has been written for use in the regular classroom, in a homogenous classroom for the gifted, or in a pullout program for the gifted. Some suggestions for introducing independent study which can be used in various settings follow:

1. The teacher may introduce independent study as a class project. The student guide may be used to teach individual skills lessons involved in independent study. After the group study is completed, students may use the guide themselves and begin an individual study.

2. The teacher may select a small group of students who may work on one project.

3. If students already have basic research skills they might all begin with an independent study.

4. One subject area, i.e., language arts can be taught through independent study.

5. One small group of students may be selected to work on individual studies.

Selecting a Topic for Study

Page 5 of the student book assists the student in selecting a topic for study. Some students do not need any assistance in making a decision. Others have a great deal of difficulty. If a student is unable to decide, additional forms in the Appendix of this book may be helpful. Students may fill out an interest inventory (Appendix 1, page 65). Parents may fill out one for their children as well (Appendix 2, page 67). A careful look at answers and a conference with the child will usually bear fruit. Children are not used to being given responsibility for their own learning and might feel uncomfortable at first. They need reassurance from their teachers and time to grow. Once the topic is selected goals for the student can be outlined.

Differentiating the Curriculum for the Gifted

The following section includes a discussion of educational principles and ideas to assist teachers in differentiating the independent study curriculum for the gifted. Its purpose is to provide teachers with ways of looking at independent studies and then selecting those ideas which they believe fit into the studies which are being developed. Some studies will lend themselves to many of the ideas discussed, while others will use very few. Teachers should base their judgments on the nature of the topic being studied, and the ability of the child. Educational ideas which have been included to differentiate the independent study curriculum for the gifted are:

1. Passow's (1982) seven guiding principles of curriculum differentiation.

2. Addressing higher cognitive levels (Bloom, 1956).

3. Basic skills and expanded basic skills (Tannenbaum, 1983).

4. Developing skills of educational connoisseurship (Eisner, 1979).

5. Developing productive thinking (Guilford, 1977).

6. Uncovering real problems and discovering solutions (Renzulli, 1982).

7. Problem solving skills (Noller, Parnes & Biondi, 1976).

Examples of typical studies done by students have been included to help demonstrate how each of these might apply.

1. Guiding Principles for Differentiating the Independent Study Curriculum (Passow, 1983)

Passow (1983) has summarized for the National Leadership Training Institute Curriculum Council seven principles on which differentiated curriculum should be based which have application for independent study.

The first stresses the need for the content of curricula to focus on more elaborate, complex and in-depth study. The nature of independent study is such that it can allow time for in-depth study. It allows study across the disciplines, as knowledge is integrated and thinking is developed. Two students began a study based on the topic of nutrition. Their research included a basic understanding of how food serves as fuel for the human body. They found out what vitamins and minerals were important to good health. They learned how emotions and psychology affect eating patterns. They met with a school nurse and monitored their eating habits for a one-week period. They met with the school nutritionist and surveyed their classmates to ascertain if students were eating balanced lunches. They found most food was being thrown away. Students had very little understanding about what good eating habits consisted of. They wrote a pamphlet for students to help educate them in this area.

The second guiding principle states that curricula for the gifted/talented should allow one to develop and apply productive thinking skills to reconceptualize existing knowledge or generate new knowledge. As students involved in an independent study complete their research they can be stimulated to address future issues. They can be encouraged to conduct surveys and draw conclusions based on findings. A student voiced an interest in history. He began with a study of World War II. He started to understand cause and effect relationships. He went on to explore the causes of war. Looking to the future, he began to assess world problems to help gain an understanding of how war could be avoided.

The third principle states that students should be allowed to explore constantly changing knowledge and information and develop the attitude that knowledge is worth pursuing in an open world. Any topic selected in an independent study program should be seen as having value. The most important message being transmitted when allowing students to pursue any area that interests them, is that knowledge is indeed worth pursuing. Students very often experience the changing nature of knowledge as they look for information in dated materials. As students learn to keep bibliographic records, they can be guided into developing an awareness of how information changes. The newspaper serves as an excellent resource. Children studying the solar system are constantly coming across the changing nature of knowledge.

Selection, and use of appropriate and specialized resources, is the fourth principle cited. Part of the procedure involved in allowing students to develop independent studies is to provide them with, and to guide them in finding appropriate resources. Taking them outside of the classroom and exposing them to a variety of appropriate experiences broadens their educational experience. This would include trips, meeting with mentors or professionals. Students may initiate their own extended experiences. Very often professionals are willing to be interviewed.

The fifth principle emphasizes self-initiated and self-directed learning and growth, should be promoted. This is the every essence of independent study. It is the child who selects the topic and formulates the design for the study with the teacher. The teacher becomes an observer and evaluates how much guidance the student needs as he conducts his research. Independence is supported and encouraged every step of the way.

The sixth principle states that curricula "should provide for the development of self-understanding and the understanding of one's relationship to persons, societal institutions, nature, and culture" (Passow, 1983, p. 9). Independent study can be an effective tool in developing leaders and leadership skills as well as an aid in the understanding of the responsibility of that role. As students become "experts" in areas and create products, these products can become part of a library. These students can be called upon to be mentors to others as they give back some of what they have acquired.

The seventh principle addresses curricula for the gifted stressing evaluation of higher-level thinking skills and excellence in performance and products. Evaluation of independent study is addressed in Section IX of this document.

2. Addressing Higher Cognitive Levels (Bloom, 1956)

Gifted students should be guided to addressing higher level thinking skills in their study. The teacher can guide the student and integrate questions and pose problems which require more complex thinking. Ability on the part of the student to address these levels is another measure of giftedness.

Teachers can help students to formulate questions for their study which address higher levels of thinking (Bloom, 1956). The levels can be outlined as follows:

a. knowledge - memorizing facts, tell, list, describe, who what, when

b. comprehension - telling about these facts in your own words, interpret, compare and contrast

c. application - using facts in new situations, demonstrate, use it to solve

d. analysis - sorting out information in new ways, looking at parts, finding important facts, how, reason, why, what are the causes

e. synthesis - designing, creating, rearranging

f. evaluation - establishing criteria and making judgments, set standards, rate, will it work, how will you decide

Gifted students need time to master information on the knowledge level as they conduct their research. The gifted child usually acquires information more rapidly and is able to move to the upper levels more quickly. Also, questions on the upper levels are usually more challenging and interesting to the gifted child. The upper three levels allow for creative thinking and risk taking, which are necessary if one is to become an inventor, a designer or a producer. The teacher can easily guide the students in incorporating questions which address analysis, synthesis or evaluation into their studies. The gifted student will welcome these kinds of questions and activities and feel stimulated.

3. Basic Skills and Expanded Skills (Tannenbaum, 1982)

Introducing students to basic skills and expanded basic skills involved in their study might be necessary for them to prepare them for careers related to their study. Basic skills and expanded basic skills are related to the nature of the work done in a particular field or profession. Introducing a student to how scientists or historians gather their data would be important to them. A student with a poetic bent should be exposed to poetry and poetry forms beyond those provided in the regular classroom. Exposure to professionals in the students' field of study to gain a broader picture of the skills involved would be enlightening. Basic skills and expanded basic skills for the gifted go beyond what we would include in the regular curriculum. Students should be introduced to the skills as needed, not as prescribed in the curriculum.

Some children begin exhibiting gifts and talents at an early age. Depending on the careers related to the area of interest, an analysis of the skills involved in that profession is necessary so that skills can be taught. An interview with the professional in that field would be most helpful. The following questions should be answered so that directions for skill development can be determined.

a. What is the nature of the work involved in a particular career? What formal schooling is required?

b. What are some of the pre-requisite areas or kinds of subjects that would serve as a good background for that topic?

c. What basic skills and expanded basic skills are necessary to performance in that field of endeavor? If one were to go through a day or week with a scientist, a doctor, or an engineer, what kinds of skills would be involved?
    - Which skills have gone into his training?
    - What kinds of interpersonal skills does that person need?
    - What written or oral skills are necessary to perform?

d. What kind of lifestyle does that person have?
    - Does he sit behind a desk?
    - Does he have regular hours?
    - Does he travel?

If possible, try to arrange to have the student spend some time with professionals, observing them in their work. The skills involved in each profession are very different. An understanding of the skills required and early development of them allows gifted children to develop at the level they are capable of. Children who evidence themselves as being scientifically precocious would be taught how to observe, record, classify, hypothesize and theorize. Prospective historians would learn how to recreate events from the past using primary, secondary and tertiary sources. Writers would be exposed to various forms and styles and learn about the writing process. Exposure and training might help to give students insights which might help them to establish a satisfying career and lifestyle.

4. Developing Skills of Educational Connoisseurship (Eisner, 1979)

Students can develop thinking skills which can help them to become educational critics or connoisseurs. Eisner (1979), in his book The Educational Imagination discusses the skills and ideas involved in educational connoisseurship and educational criticism. The type of inquiry Eisner discusses can be used in many independent studies as well as in the evaluation of the educational experience.

Eisner (1979) states:

In this sense, the critic's task is to function as a midwife to perception, to so talk about the qualities constituting the work of art that others, lacking the critic's connoisseurship, will be able to perceive the work more comprehensively.

"The end of criticism", wrote Dewey, "is the reeducation of the perception of the work of art." The critic's task in this view is not primarily the issuance of judgment, but rather the difficult task of lifting the veils that keep the eyes from seeing (p. 191).

Criticism is not viewed as a negative appraisal of something, but rather the illumination of something's qualities so that an appraisal of its value can be made. Eisner defines a connoisseur as one who knows how to look, to see, and to appreciate. Connoisseurship is the art of appreciation. Criticism is the art of disclosure. One cannot be a critic without having developed the skills of connoisseurship. The art critic describes a work so that we may see its qualities. Pervasive and component qualities are brought to our attention. The critic helps us to sharpen our perceptions. Many topics chosen for study are enhanced by the integration of Eisner's ideas. Some of the strategies that are used by Calkins (1983), in her book Lessons From a Child incorporate this kind of inquiry. Some of the questions she suggests that are posed to students follow: Which of the characters in this book seem most real to me? Why? Does the author tell me about them, or show them in action? How do the characters change throughout the story? Does the author make me want to read on? How?

26

Developing your own questions with students will assist students in defining the elements of good writing. This can serve to help develop the student as connoisseur. Which writings have survived time? Why? Which works of art have achieved greatness? Why? Why is a particular piece of music considered a masterpiece?

Not only is this approach valid for areas involving the arts but can be successfully applied to other areas as well. When given the opportunity to select a topic of study for the first time some students will select an area in the field of sports. Some of the questions to be addressed might be:

What makes a good player?

What makes a good team?

What makes a good manager?

How does one select players?

This kind of questioning forces students to think critically and analytically as they begin to peel the layers that allow one to see.

Using these skills to evaluate independent study would include another set of questions and interpretations.

What makes up an independent study?

How can it be broken down into its elements, i.e., research, organization, presentation, etc.

Which parts have I done well? Which can I improve? How do I learn best?

What criteria would I use to judge this?

Again, thinking skills are being developed which are invaluable and transferable.

5. Developing Productive Thinking (Guilford, 1977)

Guilford (1977) has developed a theory of intelligence known as the "Structure of the Intellect." It is usually represented in a cube which has three dimensions which include: (a) content or information; (b) mental operations; and (c) products. All human abilities have these three dimensions and can be classified according to the sub-categories within each dimension. Guilford believes there are many kinds of intelligence and that creative abilities seem to be concentrated in the operation of divergent production and the product of transformations. Guilford suggests that educators attempt to develop all of the abilities within his model. He recommends special attention be paid to the development of creative productive abilities in children with high I.Q.s. Students working on independent study should be encouraged to look at the possibilities and alternatives, rather than the "right answers." This helps to develop divergent thinking. Inasmuch as divergent thinking is a part of the creative process and creativity is a component of giftedness, developing divergent thinking is desirable.

6. Uncovering Real Problems and Discovering Solutions (Renzulli, 1982)

Students sometimes uncover "real problems" in their study and wish to seek solutions. Renzulli (1982) describes the characteristics of a real problem:

1. A real problem must have a personal frame of reference, since it involves an emotional or affective commitment as well as an intellectual or cognitive one.

2. A real problem does not have an existing or unique solution.

3. Calling something a problem does not necessarily make it a real problem for a given person or group.

4. The purpose of pursuing a real problem is to bring about some form of change and/or contribute something new to the sciences, the arts, or the humanities (p. 149).

According to Renzulli (1983) it is the student who selects the topic, uses appropriate investigative measures as he is the first-hand inquirer and produces new knowledge or art.

Before the teacher allows the student to become involved in the investigation of a real problem, teacher and child must ask themselves the following questions. Are there appropriate resources available to the student to perform the investigation? Are possible solutions within the sphere of influence of the child? As long as realistic expectations are established before the student begins, a study involving creative problem solving is worthwhile. The teacher might well have to lay the appropriate groundwork before the student begins.

The student will have to be guided in using appropriate investigative techniques as well as using the Creative Problem Solving Methodology (Noller, Parnes, & Biondi, 1976). The outline for this process is included in Appendix 4, p. 70) so that the teacher may instruct the student in the use of the process.

7. Problem Solving Skills, (Noller, Parnes & Biondi, 1976)

Noller et al. (1976), in their "Creative Actionbook," describe a method for problem solving which can assist in problem solving. The Creative Problem Solving Model provides a structured method for approaching problems in an imaginative way. It is comprised of 5 steps which include fact finding, problem finding, idea finding, solution finding, and acceptance finding. Purposes of the model are, (1) to provide a sequential process that will enable an individual to being with a "mess" and arrive at a creative solution, and (2) to enhance an individual's overall creative behavior. The process stresses divergent production. As students come across problems in their study they can be taught this method. Possible solutions can be sought as children develop divergent thinking and problem solving skills.

Project or Product Development

Developing a project or product is an important part of the independent study process. the student book includes a list of suggestions for designing projects. There are several reasons why project development is important:

1. After students complete their research, preparing a project forces them to see if their research is adequate. The independent study process includes keeping track of notes and keeping an accurate bibliography. The student now has the opportunity to understand the reasons for this and value it.

2. Organizational skills are observed or taught. This can be an asset to the student in future research.

3. Students are encouraged to make their own decisions and choices in project development. They have an opportunity to design a product or presentation that they can be proud of.

4. Students have talents and abilities which do not always appear in the research segment of independent study. When students have choices, artistic or dramatic talents sometimes surface.

5. Communication skills, either written or verbal can be developed and refined.

6. After projects are completed, appropriate audiences for works can be taught. These may range from:
   a. Sharing their work with peers.
   b. Arranging a display for the school.
   c. Setting up a fair for parents.
   d. Teaching what has been learned in other settings, i.e., a 5th grader might teach principles of electronics to 7th graders, or a 4th grader might teach small groups of 2nd graders how to program a computer.
   e. Sending work to publishers.

7. After a project is completed evaluation can take place. This allows students to look at what they have done in terms of their own talents and abilities. They can assess independent study as an appropriate educational opportunity assisting them in becoming educational connoisseurs.

8. When students receive positive feedback and feel successful, their self-esteem can be enhanced and their motivation to continue learning may increase.

9. Products can become part of the classroom or school library. Students have now become producers and they can be called upon in the future to serve as mentors to others. Leadership skills are sometimes developed as they take on this new role.

Summary

As the teacher begins to work with students involved in independent study, the following should be kept in mind:

1. Every child should be considered for opportunities for selecting independent study as a curricular option.

2. The teacher assumes the role of facilitator and observes behaviors.

3. The teacher notes behaviors which are indicators of giftedness.

4. The teacher gives the student as much support as is necessary so that the student does not become discouraged or frustrated. The teacher assists the student in incorporating strategies which differentiate the curriculum, i.e., using general curriculum principles, using higher level thought processes, understanding the nature of the discipline(s), teaching research skills, basic skills and expanded basic skills, integrating skills of connoisseurship, or uncovering real problems and seeking for solutions.

5. The teacher and student locate materials and assistance necessary for project development. The teacher assists in finding appropriate audiences for the student's work.

V

Troubleshooting Some Common Problems

The purpose of this section is to describe different kinds of reactions students might have to independent study and to offer suggestions for dealing with problems when they arise.

Getting Students Started

Students are generally not used to making their own decisions regarding curriculum. Some students select a topic immediately and others experience difficulty. Some ways which might prove helpful might be: have the student fill out an interest inventory (Appendix 1, p.65), have the parents fill one out for their child (Appendix 2, p.67), ask students to write an autobiography about themselves upon their retirement. Send them to the school library and have them browse around to see if they like books in a particular section. Using one or all of this might help to provide additional information and insight to assist in topic selection.

Topic Selection Problems

Student not Interested in Topic Selected

Students should be allowed to change topics as long as this does not become a repeated pattern. Depending on the characteristics of each individual child, teachers must use their own discretion in determining whether or not the student is avoiding research. If a student has already expended time and energy with the topic, he/she should be encouraged to summarize work completed and feelings about the experience. If a student attempts a few different topics and shows no interest, independent study might not be appropriate at this time.

Student Selects a Topic Which is Too Narrow

The student should be allowed to begin and should soon discover that materials are limited. The teacher may then guide him in broadening it. A student beginning with the study of the condor may go on to endangered species. A student studying star formation may extend the study to include black holes.

Student Selects a Topic Which Student has Already Exhausted

Student has already read anything and everything that is available and has an in-depth knowledge of the topic to begin with. Different directions may be taken with the student. The student may be asked to choose between selecting another topic or continuing with the topic so that the teacher can guide the student with:

a.   gathering and recording the information so far obtained,

b.   finding additional human resources and places to visit,

c.   seeing if there are basic skills or expanded basic skills that should be taught as they relate to the study,

d.   asking students questions which are thought provoking and address higher level thought processes,

e.   looking for "real problems" connected with the study and see if student can begin to look for solutions,

f.   looking for social issues and solutions.

Student Selects a Topic Which is Too Broad
i.e. Music, World History, Sports, World War II, etc.

The teacher should discuss with the student the vastness of the topic and guide him/her in narrowing it. A student might begin studying World War II. After beginning the research, the student might find that studying one battle is sufficient. There is nothing wrong with a student attempting to cover a broad topic as long as the teacher monitors progress and student does not become overwhelmed. The teacher may suggest that the student narrow the topic.

Student Selects a Topic Which is Extremely Unusual and for Which Information is Not Readily Available

The student might:

a. select another related area of interest and become involved in additional research as he/she waits for information or interviews,

b. become actively involved in trying to find information and resources,

c. rely on human resources for information.

As long as the student is aware of the "problems" involved in studying a topic of this nature, he/she should be allowed to do so. Taking a chance often yields exciting rewards.

Student Selects Topic - Reading Material is on Too High a Level

Student selects a topic and most of the information is on too difficult a level for him, e.g., nuclear energy or lasers. There may be some materials on an elementary level but much of what is available might come from governmental agencies, magazines, or difficult readings. It might be necessary to assist the student yourself, or have mentors, family members, or high school students spend time and discuss the material with him/her.

Student Selects A Study for Which He/She Does Not Have Skills

Students sometimes wish to become involved in a study and project for which they do not have basic skills and knowledge, e.g., building a robot. Students must first find out about principles on which robots work. They must discuss with professionals scientific principles and actual skills necessary to build a robot, i.e., understand circuitry and soldering. They must first acquire the basic knowledge and skills necessary before actually building the robot.

Student Selects a Topic Because a friend is Studying it

Some students work best with a partner and some students need to "get their feet wet" through someone else's interest. Much can be accomplished and gained from allowing this to take place. Once students become more comfortable with independent study, they often select a topic of their own.

Student Selects a Topic That is of a Sensitive Nature

Sometimes students will select a topic which might be sensitive such as divorce or child abuse. These interests may arise from the student's environment or may be the result of natural curiosity. Parents and administrators should be advised of the child's interest. Their help might be enlisted. The study can be approached objectively.

Student Selects a Topic Which Includes Manipulatives Such as Batteries and Bulbs

Student only wants to experiment and does not want to do research or write up the experiments. Inventing and designing can be productive learning but learning to record it properly is part of a professional's work. A certain amount of patience and instruction as to appropriate procedure is necessary. If the student appears gifted but immature, it might be wise to compromise. Recording one out of every three experiments or recording work verbally on a tape recorder might suffice.

Project Anxiety

Students who have worked with independent study and have developed projects sometimes become overly concerned with the product before they even begin their research. Teachers may assure students that a project will emerge after research is completed.

Student is Difficult to Motivate

Interest inventories and trips to the library have not been successful. Try to provide exposure experiences for these students. Bring them in touch with speakers and places which might be stimulating. Bring in junior high or high school students to speak on topics of their own interest. Not only might the student become interested but the older student might continue to serve as a mentor. Not every student will succeed in an independent study program. Sometimes taking a "furlough" from independent study is indicated.

Student Appears to have Low Self-esteem

Point out their successes. Establishing realistic goals on the way to great expectations and recognizing "smaller" accomplishments may aid in the development of a healthy self-concept. Help students to enjoy and appreciate "what they have already accomplished" before reaching for the next step. Encourage them to become risk takers. Mistakes are not mistakes but can be viewed as learning experiences. What will happen if I _____? What is the worst that will result? What is the best? Help them to turn negative situations into positive ones. Tension can inhibit action and creative thought. Help them to deal with stress creatively. Teaching students relaxation exercises or visualization techniques can be useful.

Student has Difficulty Accepting Criticism

Gifted children may be highly sensitive to criticism. Most of their work in the classroom has always been praised. Having students refine their work may be more difficult for them than expected. A gentle reassuring hand guiding them and an explanation of the purpose for the refinements can help students to accept suggestions for change. Emphasis should be placed on making "the best better."

Teachers may begin to observe children who exhibit some behaviors which are indicators of giftedness. Not every student will "succeed" in an independent study program. Some students will express sheer joy when given the opportunity to investigate areas of interest and will exhibit tremendous task commitment, motivation, and creativity. They will have the opportunity to exhibit advanced thinking abilities. They will recognize problems, identify issues and produce creative ideas and projects. Others will find it tedious. Being identified as gifted does not guarantee success and does not guarantee that the child is gifted. Criteria used to identify the gifted child are not totally accurate. Sometimes good lesson learners are identified who may not be gifted. Some students need time to grow.

VI.

Typical Independent Studies Done By Students

Sample Topics Chosen by Students

Chemistry
King Tut
Gerbils
Hamsters
Medieval Knights
Football
Olympics
Solar system
Dolphins
Whales
Birds
Greek Mythology
Animation
Medical Technology
Claymation
Television Production
Allergies
ESP
The Human Body
Picasso
Art
Surrealism
World's Major Religions

The Skeletal System
The Brain
Women's Rights
Rabbits
Civil War
Politics
Lasers
Weather Disasters
Dogs
Reptiles
Ants
The Heart
Movie Critiquing
Computers in the Schools
Ballet
Child Abuse
Law
The Supreme Court
Hypnotism
Biorhythms
Codes and Cyphers
Divorce
Computers

Examples of Studies Done by Students

The following examples have been included to illustrate how some of the educational ideas have been integrated into studies completed by students.

Computers

In this study the student selected the topic of computers. To begin with, knowledge and research skills were addressed. Resources used included books, slide sound programs, school personnel, a company where computers are made and a local computer store. He met each week with a high school student who taught him programming in BASIC. The student learned about all of the different jobs that are computer related and the preparation and training for each. The student then began to explore the uses of computers and the ways they were and could be used in schools. He began to learn computer programming skills. He looked at commercial programs being packaged for computer assisted instruction. Higher level thought processes were addressed as the student analyzed computer capabilities and needs of different populations. He began to establish a list of criteria necessary for him to decide which computer would best serve his needs. He became aware of the fact that computers were not being used in the schol and began to question why. The teacher acquainted him with the problem solving methodology. The teacher arranged for him to meet with the Principal of the school and the Assistant Superintendent in his school district. Administrators explained that they wanted to see computers used more, but seemed to be getting resistance from the staff. With the permission from the administration and a cover letter from them he distributed a questionnaire to the staff to see if he could ascertain the causes of any resistance. He analyzed the results and, based on the data he received, he thought of creative ways of assisting teachers to feel more comfortable with computers. He outlined his ideas in a letter to the Principal and Assistant Superintendent. The following year many of his ideas were implemented.

Women's Rights

This student voiced an interest in women's rights. She began by reading books. She researched the history of the women's rights movement in books and articles. She interviewed a female judge and two female administrators.

She discovered females who were married, had children and had experienced a certain amount of conflict about not being able to spend as much time with their children as they would have liked to. She became concerned about the effect this might be having on children of working parents. She designed a survey which she disseminated to all fourth and fifth grade students in her school to determine how many children lived in homes where both parents worked and how this was being handled. She also wanted to know if any of the children were feeling adverse effects as a result. She analyzed the results of her survey and discovered that some children were experiencing difficulties and were not verbalizing them to their parents. She began to explore ways that partners in a marriage might avoid this problem with their children. She wrote a report on women's rights but she did not attempt to disseminate any of the findings of her survey. Her own thinking was expanded and she began formulating ideas on how she might achieve happiness and success in her own life. In the future, she might address the issue of helping others.

Football

This student wanted to study football. He already had an enormous amount of information about the game. He began studying its history using books. He read magazines and newspaper articles and wrote a letter to a sportswriter from a daily newspaper. The sportswriter came to class to meet with the student and to discuss sports with him. The newswriter discussed with the student what team play was about, how important the roles of the coach and manager were, and how players were drafted. They discussed the difference between offensive and defensive players and began analyzing the characteristics of each. They discussed game strategies and strengths and weaknesses of specific teams. The student began watching games and reporting as a critic would. He collected and read accounts of the games in the newspaper and rewrote those he thought should be. He completed a project which included a book of his writings and predictions for the following year.

Cats

The student selected cats as a topic of study. She began her research with books and pamphlets on the care and feeding of cats. She was given information on the classification system and was introduced to the nature of biology. She was taken to a local veterinary hospital where she interviewed the vet and witnessed an operation of a cat being spayed. A representative from the Humane Society was invited to speak. She became aware of the problems caused for cats when adults are irresponsible and abandon their animals, as well as the problems that abandoned animals cause. She wrote an opinion paper incorporating some suggestions as to how some of these problems might be solved. She wrote a book about her research and designed a pamphlet which she disseminated at a project fair held in her school to encourage others to become aware of the situation. The following year she became a mentor to another student.

Civil War

A student who expressed an interest in the Civil War, upon beginning his research, came to realize that the topic was extremely broad. He decided to focus in on major battles. The student was introduced to the nature of the discipline and exposed to the way a historian conducts his research. He met with a high school history teacher, a local doctor and a high school student who were "Civil War buffs." He met each week with a high school student, in the high school library, who helped him review microfilm copies of the New York Times at that particular time. He began to interpret the data establishing the cause and effect relationships. He made a video tape using audio visual materials explaining the events that led to the Civil War.

Claymation - Film Animation Using Clay Figures

Two students expressed an interest in claymation. Students watched many different films which used this technique and began to understand its elements. They established criteria to help them to evaluate the use of clay figures in films they watched and wrote summaries for those they thought were excellent explaining what it was that made them so. They met with the Audio Visual Director in the school district who assisted them and gave them guidelines so that they might film an original work. They brainstormed to decide what kind of film they would make. They designed characters, sets and scenery and wrote a script. They filmed their work at the high school film studio. Their work was thought to be superior by the Audio Visual Director and is being used as an example when he teaches both the elementary and high school level. The Director is also exploring the possibility of entering the film in a contest.

Sculpture

This student chose sculpture as his topic. He began by reading about the different kinds of sculpture. He became interested in wood carving. A history teacher at the high school was an accomplished wood carver. He met with the student explaining how a wood carver works and showed him examples of his own work. The student found that this was not of interest to him but that the work of a particular sculptress who worked with wood pieces appealed to him. An administrator in the school district was a former art teacher. She became his mentor for the year and met with him on a weekly basis. They visisted museums together and discussed the works. The student was exposed to the nature of the arts and their role in society. The student began defining what it was that made a sculpture a work of art. He began to explore some of the problems the sculptress faces as she works and began to design his own original works. They were presented at a project fair and were kept on display in the school.

Lasers

This student was interested in lasers. He began reading about lasers and found that some of the material was too difficult for him because of the mathematical theories involved. The student met with the high school physics teacher who spent time with him explaining how the theories of light refraction operated. The teacher gave the student a laser and a set of laser experiments to use. The student was taken to a local hospital where he met with a doctor who used lasers in his work. The student witnessed membranes being removed after a cataract operation performed with a laser. He interviewed the doctor and was referred to a number of articles which were extremely helpful. The student was introduced to the nature of scientific inquiry and performed his experiments the way a scientist would. The student began to address possible future uses for the laser. The student lectured and demonstrated the use of the laser to classes at different levels in the school. The student was in fifth grade when he completed the study. His interest has continued. He is now entering high school and is considering opthalmology as a career.

VII.

Developing Resources

Developing Outside Resources for Independent Study

Students generally bring a wide variety of interests to independent study. The school's resources and those to which teachers have access outside the school are often inadequate. Developing additional resources to meet students' needs is often necessary. Following are some suggestions.

People

Parents. The talents, interests, and hobbies of students' parents can be an excellent resource. Most parents feel gratified when they are invited to become part of the educational process. Many are already looking for outlets for their surplus energies. Housewives are eager to demonstrate their value outside their homes. Working mothers and fathers are delighted to share their professional expertise. Have all parents of students complete the resources development mentor questionnaire included in Appendix 3, p. 69).

School staff. Teachers have areas of expertise and hobbies which they are often happy to share. Classroom teachers enjoy becoming part of a program for a gifted child.

Other students. Students in other grades or those who have studied with you in the past are wonderful mentors for children.

Other teachers involved in independent study. Exchanging ideas and resources with teachers in your school or in other schools can prove very worthwhile. It may be possible to join forces with teachers in other school systems. Some educational organizations have teacher sharing groups.

Local businessmen. Local businessmen are usually eager to become involved in the education of children and will make their resources available.

Specialists in your school system. Heads of departments and administrators have expertise and hobbies they enjoy sharing.

Career development personnel. Guidance counselors usually possess a broad range of knowledge and can refer you to specific resources, e.g., community clubs, the Boy Scouts, the Girl Scouts, 4-H, and other community groups. Staffs are well informed and they often provide free or low-cost literature.

Local politicians. Elected officials are always eager to participate in the process of education. Councilmen, congressmen, and senators often meet with students.

Grandparents. Retired grandparents are often willing to serve.

Community Resources

Local libraries. Take a trip to the local library to acquaint students with the references and other sources of information available there. Not all children are aware of the wide variety of materials that libraries collect. Most children are familiar with encyclopedias and almanacs. Draw their attention to alternative sources of information, such as The New York Times Obituaries Index and Who's Who. The latter is doubly valuable because it provides readers with the addresses of famous people students' may be studying. Students should also be shown how to use the microfilm and microfiche collections.

Library networks. Some local libraries have established a central network of resources for their communities. People involved in such networks are ready to share their knowledge on particular topics free of charge or for a small fee. Some have these on computer.

Local universities. Universities can provide access not only to highly knowledgeable people, but also to sophisticated research facilities.

Local hospitals. Many hospitals provide guided tours for students and staff who are willing to share.

Large companies and organizations. Many profit and non-profit organizations offer tours of their facilities or booklets of public information. They may also provide special educational programs or speakers who will talk with your students.

Local Agencies or Groups

Local organizations for gifted and telented children. These are excellent sources of information and support. Become affiliated with your local organization, or, if your community lacks such a group, help get one started.

Government agencies. Government agencies often provide free or lost cost literature.

Special interest clubs. Check your local newspapers for notification of meetings and exhibits which might be relevant to studies.

Senior citizen's groups. Senior citizens have plenty of time on their hands, many experiences to share, and a desire to demonstrate that they are still valuable and needed members of the community.

Special Written or Audio-Visual Materials

Film lists. Aside from the films available in the school, local libraries may have a film collection of their own. Companies, manufacturers, or other corporations, such as the Cancer Society, the Humane Society, Shell Oil Company, and Bell Telephone put their own films together for free distribution.

Slide-sound programs. In addition to the programs which school districts already own, companies will send programs on approval. These can be ordered for specific students. Recommendations for purchase can be made to the district.

Classified Advertisements. Students can learn a lot just by examining the classified ads in the newspapers. These ads are likely to include listings for jobs in the field that are of interest to a student. Because the ads usually provide a description of what the job entails, required qualifications and experience, and approximate salary, a student can combine the information from several listings to reach some generalizations about a profession.

Newspapers. It is a good idea to have at least one daily newspaper in the classroom so that students can learn to look for current information relating to their topics. Children usually love receiving a newspaper and are eager to find ways of using it. Newspapers often provide special services, such as a speaker's bureau, when their paper is subscribed to.

Your own files. Start a collection of newspaper clippings, magazine articles, and pamphlets. Catalog them so that your students can find information more easily.

The Yellow Pages. Use the Yellow Pages to find companies who employ people with expertise in fields which your students are studying. People are often willing to help.

Audio-Visual Tapes. It is possible to establish your own library of audio-visual tapes. Keeping a supply of blank tapes on hand and either taping programs yourself or asking others to tape for you will expand your resource library and help provide for your students who prefer visual materials.

These are only some of the ways in which you can help develop resources for your students. You can continually supplement the list with your own additions.

Resource Bibliography

General Independent Study Resources

Cardozo, P., & Menten, T. (1975). The whole kids catalog. New York: Bantam

Wurman, R.S. (Ed.) (1972). Yellow pages of learning resources. Philadelphia: A Group for Environmental Education.

Designing Audio-Visual Products

Green, L., & Denjerink, D. (1982). 501 ways to use the overhead projector. Colorado: Libraries Unlimited.

Heinich, R., & Molenda, M. (1982). Instructional media and the new technologies of instruction. New York: John Wiley & Sons.

Kemp, J.E. (1980). Planning and producing audio visual materials. New York: Harper & Row.

Kodak Picture and Audiovisual Markets Division of Eastman Kodak. Kodak: slides with a purpose. Rochester, NY: Author.

Platt, J. (Ed.) (1973). Young animators v. their discoveries. New York: Praeger Publishers.

Technifax (1969). A teacher's guide to overhead projection. Mt. Holyoke, MA: The Plastic Coating Corp.

Designing Questionnairs and Surveys

Bialock, H. (1960). Social statistics. New York: McGraw-Hill.

Oppenheim, A.N. (1966). Questionnaire design and attitude measurement. New York: Basic Books.

Shaw, M., & Wright, J. (1967). Scales for the measurement of attitudes. New York: McGraw-Hill.

Smith, G.M. (1962). A simplified guide to statistics (4th ed.). New York: Holt, Rinehart, & Winston.

Creative Problem Solving

Adams, J. (1974). Conceptual blockbusting. San Francisco, CA: Freeman Press.

deMille, R. (1973). Put your mother on the ceiling: Children's imagination games. New York: Viking.

Eberle, B. (1982). Visual Thinking. Buffalo, NY: D.O.K.

Eberle, B., & Stanish, B. (1980). CPS for kids. Buffalo, NY: D.O.K.

Eberle, R.F. (1971). Scamper: Games for imagination development. Buffalo, NY: D.O.K.

Noller R. (1977). Scratching the surface of creative problem solving. Buffalo, NY: D.O.K.

Noller, R., Parnes, S., & Biondi, A. (1976). Creative actionbook. New York: Scribners.

Parnes, S.J. (1981). The magic of your mind. Buffalo, NY: Creative Education Foundation.

Parnes, S., Noller, R., & Biondi, A. (Eds.) (1977). Guide to creative action. New York: Scribners.

Math and Logic

Buckeye, Euebank, Ginther. (1971). A cloudburst of math lab experiments. Troy, MI: Midwest Publications.

Duedney, E.E. (1967). 536 puzzles and curious problems. New York: Charles Scribners Sons.

Kordemsky, B.A. (1972). The Moscow puzzles. New York: Charles Scribners Sons.

Matthews G. Nuffield mathematics project. New York: John Wiley. (A British program for ages 5-12)

Noller, R., Heintz, R., & Blaeuer, D. (1978). Creative problem solving in mathematics. Buffalo, NY: D.O.K.

Reading and Language Arts

Calkins, L.M. (1983). Lessons from a child. New Hampshire: Heinemann Educational Books.

Gordon, W.J., & Poze, T. (1972). Strange and familiar. Cambridge, MA: Porpoise Books.

Kaplan, S.N., & Kaplan, J.G. (1969). Keys to understanding mankind: Open-end reading task cards. Monterey Park, CA: Creative Teacher Press.

Witty, P. (Ed.) (1971). Reading for the gifted and creative student. Newark, DE: International Reading Association.

Zinsser, W. (1983). On writing well. New York: Harper & Row.

Science

Allison, L. (1976). Blood and guts: A working guide to your own insides. Boston: Little, Brown & Co.

Carin, A., & Sand, R. (1970). Teaching science through discovery. Columbus, OH: Charles Merrill.

DeVito, A., & Krockover, G. (1976). Creative sciencing II, Ideas and activities for teachers and children. boston: Little, Brown & Co.

McGavack, L., & LaSalle, D. (1971). Crystals, insects, and unknown objects: A creative approach to the teaching of science to intermediate school children. New York: John Day.

Sund, R., Tillery, B., & Trowbridge, L. (1975). Investigate and discover elementary science lessons. Boston: Allyn & Bacon.

Social Studies

American Genealogical Research Institute Staff. (1975). How to trace your family tree: A complete and easy to understand guide for the beginner. Garden City, NY: Doubleday & Co.

Carr, E. H. (1962). What is history? New York: Alfred A. Knopf.

Gottschak, L. (1969). Understanding history: A primer of historical method (2nd ed.) New York: Alfred A. Knopf.

Raths, L., Harmin, M., & Simon, S. (1966). Values and teaching: working with values in the classroom. Columbus, OH: Carles Merrill.

Simon, S., & Clark, J. (1975). Beginning values clarification: Strategies for the classroom. San Diego, CA: Pennant.

Simon, S., Howe, L., & Kirschenbaum, H. (1972). Values clarification: A handbook of practical strategies for teachers and students. New York: Hart.

Weitzman, D. (1975). My backyard history book. Boston: Little, Brown.

Winks, R. (1968). The historian as detective. New York: Harper.

Youngers, J.C., & Aceti, J.F. (1969). Simulation games for social studies. Dansville, NY: The Instructor Publications.

Zuckerman, D.W., & Horn, R.E. (Eds.) (1973). The guide to simulations/education and training. Lexington, MA: Information Resources.

Catalogs or Materials Appropriate for the Gifted

Since new materials are constantly being developed and updated, teachers can request free catalogues and can be placed on mailing lists. A list of distributors who publish suitable catalogues or materials follows:

A. W. Peller and Associates Inc.
249 Goffle Road
Hawthorne, NJ 17505

Carolina Biological Supply Co.
Burlington, NC 27215

The Center for Humanities Inc.
Two Holland Avenue
White Plains, NY 10603

Creative Learning Systems International
Dept. 3
936 C Street
San Diego, CA 92101

Dandy Lion Publications
P. O. Box 190, Dept. FD
San Luis Obiispo, CA 93406

D.O.K. Publishers
P. O. Box 605
East Aurora, NY 14052

Elementary Science Study
Webster Division
McGraw Hill Book Company
1221 Avenue of the Americas
New York, NY 10020

Guidance Associates
Communications Park
Box 3000
Mount Kisco, NY 10549

Midwest Publications
P. O. Box 448
Pacific Grove, CA 93950

Opportunities for Learning Inc.
20417 Nordhoff Street
Dept. NH
Chalsworth, CA 91311

Resources for the Gifted Inc.
P. O. Box 15050
Phoenix, AZ 85060

Sunburst Communications
Room NH 939
39 Washington Avenue
Pleasantville, NY 10570

Synergetics
P. O. Box 84
East Windsor Hill, CT 06028

Trillium Press
Box 921
Madison Square Station
New York, NY 10159

Just as students must learn to experiment and become "risk takers" so must teachers. Developing appropriate and sufficient resources for an independent study program takes a lot of time and patience. Testing new materials and having students evaluate them with teachers helps to develop the skills of educational connoisseurship which are so desirable.

VIII.

Independent Study Program Management

Developing Independent Study as a Curricular Option

Many demands and contraints are placed on teachers today both in the regular classroom or in special settings. The teacher should assess the ability of the class to do independent work as well as their knowledge of research skills. Since this guide is intended for use in regular classrooms, in homogeneous classes for the gifted, and pullout programs for the gifted, introduction to independent study can take many forms. The teacher must make the decision as to which one to begin with based on the class population.

1. The teacher may use the student guide as a teaching guide and conduct a group independent study with the entire class. After the students learn the skills involved the teacher may:
    a. allow all of the students to begin an independent study,
    b. break the class into groups and have each group select a topic,
    c. select particular students and allow them to select a topic to study,
    d. have students self-select and allow those who wish to do so select a study.

2. Establish a small group of able students in the class. Review research skills and encourage them to use the Student Resource Book.

3. Students who have been in programs for the gifted who are familiar with research skills can be given the Student Resource Book to use at the outset.

4. Offer independent study to anyone who wishes it. Give them the student book. Set up appointments for private conferences.

Teachers should begin to examine the different programming options which can be utilized to provide independent study. Following is a chart which might help them to generate some other ideas. Program alternatives can be mixed, matched and combined.

Independent Study

With Whom	Where	At What Time
Classroom teacher	In the classroom	One period per day Regular class-time
Other teacher	At home	Before school
High School Student	In another teacher's room	After school
Peers		
Librarians	In any room in the building	Weekends
School specialists	At someone's place of business	Lunchtime
Senior citizens		
Community residents		
Business people		
Administrators		
College students		
University staff		
Educational television		

Some other suggestions follow:

1.   Set aside a special time each week for independent study.

2.   Set up an independent study interest center.

3.   Allow students to work on independent study whenever their regular classroom work is completed.

4.   Compact an area of the curriculum to make room for independent study (Renzulli, 1977). This involves examining each area of the regular curriculum in which a youngster shows a particular strength. Look at achievement tests and previous records. If a student shows proficiency in a specific content area, a diagnosis of needs in that area should take place. If the student has already mastered all that is planned in the curriculum, this time can be allotted to independent study. If there are small gaps in learning, just those should be taught, leaving time for independent study. Join forces with other teachers.

5.   Specialize and set apart a time during the week when one teacher works with independent study. Program management should also include ways of finding intellectual and interest mates for students. This may take time at first but becomes easier as time goes on and resources are extended. Ideally, all teachers should be sharing resources and ideas. Teachers may send notices through the school asking for resources on special topics. They might ask the local newspaper to write an article about the studies being undertaken by students asking for help. Special interest clubs in the community may exist. Newspapers usually give listings of meetings and exhibits. If one does not exist maybe one can be formed. Organizing interest clubs within the school and integrating students also serves to bring students together, i.e., chess, dungeons and dragons, stamps, rocks, etc. The boundaries of the classroom for both teachers and students need to be broken down to extend learning experiences and resources to wherever they might be available.

IX.

Evaluation of Independent Study

Selecting Procedures

The purpose of this section is to provide ideas for teachers to assist them in designing evaluation measures which are appropriate for independent study and to provide some examples. In order to evaluate what is happening appropriately, it is important to examine goals established at the outset to determine which aspects of independent study curriculum are to be evaluated. Before one begins selecting appropriate evaluation procedures, the purpose of evaluation must be examined. After the goals outlined initially have been addressed, the goal of evaluation itself should next be looked at. How might we assess what has taken place so that we might improve upon it?

Some types of evaluation one might undertake might be:

1. Students can evaluate their own growth as a result of their experience with independent study.

2. The teacher can evaluate the child's development in specific areas as the study is completed.

3. Student products can be evaluated.

4. Growth in content areas can be evaluated.

5. The teacher might evaluate independent study as a curricular option.

Evaluation procedures may take many different forms. Following are a list of independent study goals and of evaluation procedures (based partly on Wolf, 1979).

Goals to be Evaluated

Possible Evaluation Procedures

Goals to be Evaluated	Formal Test	Objective Self-Report	Written Report	Oral Questioning	Planned Observation (Checklist)	Product or Performance Observed (Rated)	Incidental Observation	Anecdotal Record
Learn steps of I.S.		x		x	x	x		
Learn Research Skills	x	x	x	x	x	x		
Extend Resources Outside of Class		x		x	x	x		
Organize Work				x	x		x	x
See More Than One Solution to a Problem	x	x		x	x	x	x	x
Generate more Creative Ideas for projects		x		x	x	x	x	
Thinker	x	x		x	x	x	x	x
Feel Better About Self	x	x		x				
Find Other People With Interests		x		x				
Learn more about ____	x		x	x				
Become more of a leader								
Become an independent learner		x				x	x	x
Accept responsibility for Work		x		x		x	x	
Take more chances experiment		x		x	x	x	x	
Become aware of strengths and weaknesses		x	x					
Learn to work alone		x			x			
Speak in front of small groups					x			
Make a large group presentation					x			
Learn to make decisions		x		x	x	x	x	x
Learn to judge usefulness of facts		x		x	x	x	x	

Not all of the evaluation procedures listed will be suitable for all the educational goals listed. The teacher has to match the appropriate evaluation procedure to the specific goal being considered.

The essence of evaluation is to assist both teacher and student in finding out what "works" and what needs to be improved. Evaluation should be the beginning of change in redesign if necessary.

Sample Evaluation Forms

On the following pages are sample evaluation forms which teachers might find helpful. Teachers can begin to design evaluation forms for their own needs as time goes on.

Sample Evaluation Form #1

INDEPENDENT STUDY

NAME _____ DATE _____

Now that we have reached mid-year, we would like to evaluate the Independent Study to date. In order to continually improve our program, and change it whenever necessary to meet your needs, we need as much feed-back as possible from you, the student, about your progress.

Listed below are a number of statements which pertain to your work in the Independent Study. Please indicate the degree to which each describes your progress by placing a check mark in one of the boxes following each statement. There are five possible responses where a 1 means "not at all" or "no progress" and a 5 means "very much" or "excellent progress."

Please be sure to reply to the statements at the end and add any additional comments.

	Yes			No	
	1	2	3	4	5
1) You have a more positive attitude toward yourself.					
2) You have a more positive attitude toward school.					
3) You are more willing to participate in discussions.					
4) You have developed new ideas and/or concepts.					
5) You feel you have developed a wider range of interests.					
6) Extent to which you enjoy being with students doing independent study.					
7) You are learning to work more independently.					
8) You are learning to accept other's opinions and share work and ideas.					
9) You take full advantage of the opportunities offered.					
10) You are learning different approaches to solving problems.					

I prefer Independent Studies_____ Group Mini-Studies_____ Centers.

Topics of special interest to me are:

COMMENTS (you may use the back of this paper)

Sample Evaluation Form #2

Student Questionnaire to Assess Independent Study as an Appropriate Curricular Option

NAME_____ DATE_____

1. I feel better about myself because of my
    accomplishments in the independent study program.   yes_____ no_____

2. I would like independent study to be incorporated
    in my future program.   yes_____ no_____

3. Check one: I enjoy_____ locating resources. I have difficulty_____ locating
    resources.

4. Check if it applies to you:

    _____ I have learned how to narrow my research.

    _____ I have learned how to broaden my research.

    _____ I have been exposed to ways of finding information other than
             books.

    _____ I look forward to learning and doing research as a result of my
             independent study.

5. Check one: I feel it is important_____ unimportant_____ to spend part of my
    school time with other children who have common interest.

6. I have used resources other than books. (Check those you have used)

    _____ interviews   _____ other (specify):

    _____ trips   _____

    _____ experimenting   _____

7. Doing a project allows me to use original ideas
    and be creative.   yes_____ no_____

8. I believe my creative abilities have been improved
    as a result of doing an independent study.   yes_____ no_____

9. I enjoy working with other students involved in
    independent study.   yes_____ no_____

10. I feel better about my research skills.   yes_____ no_____

11. I enjoy learning more since I completed an
    independent study.   yes_____ no_____

12. I would like to share my project or research (check as many of the following as apply to you):

_____ At a project fair

_____ With one other student

_____ With my class

_____ With other classes

_____ I do not like sharing at all

13. I feel this way about my research (check one):

_____ I am doing a good job

_____ I am doing just what is required

_____ I hope never to do research again

14. Independent study (check one):

_____ Keeps my interest

_____ Helps me to do research in other areas

_____ Is boring

_____ Is difficult

15. I did my research because (check one):

_____ It was a topic I was interested in

_____ My teacher would be upset if I did not do it

_____ I could think of nothing else

_____ My friend chose to do it

16. I feel this way about independent projects (check one):

_____ I can't wait to do another one

_____ I would like to try another one someday

_____ It was o.k. but I would not be eager to do it again

_____ They are not worth the trouble

17. I am better able to evaluate the things I do   yes_____ no_____

18. I can make independent study better by:

19. Others can help me by:

20. Comments:

Sample Evaluation Form #3

Evaluation of Product to be Used by Student and/or Peer

NAME_____DATE_____

Product:

Rate each of the items according to the following scale

       0 - Not observed at all

       1 - Fair - could be impved a lot

       2 - Very good

       3 - Excellent

1. _____ The product is attractive.

2. _____ The product demonstrates in-depth knowledge of the topic.

3. _____ The product is well organized.

4. _____ The product shows use of extended resources.

5. _____ The bibliography shows wide selection of books and periodicals.

6. _____ The product is clear, meaningful, interesting and understandable.

7. _____ The product is imaginative and creative.

The best part of this product was:

I would like to see the following changed:

Sample Evaluation Form #4

Teacher Objective Report of Student Growth

Student Name_____ Date_____

Please evaluate the pupil by placing the letter a, b, or c on the line beside each item according to the scale below. Think of the student in relation to performance at the beginning of the independent study experience.

a – Diminishing   b – about the same   c – increased

1. _____ Interest in school.
2. _____ Knowledge of topic being studied.
3. _____ Ability to make decisions.
4. _____ Ability to see relationships.
5. _____ Ability to solve problems.
6. _____ Knowledge of basic skills.
7. _____ Intellectual curiosity.
8. _____ Ability to formulate questions
9. _____ Ability to work independently.
10. _____ Motivation toward learning.
11. _____ Status in peer group.
12. _____ Leadership ability.
13. _____ Ability to evaluate self.
14. _____ Research skills.

Sample Evaluation Form #5

Teacher Anecdotal Report of Student Growth

Name of Student _____ Date _____

Topic studied:

Research skills:

Organizational skills:

Task orientation:

Leadership qualities:

Creative abilities:

Divergent thinking abilities:

Special strengths:

Improvements needed:

Research skills:

Organizational skills:

In-depth study:

Project development:

Sample Evaluation Form #6

Teacher Objective Report of Student in Content Area: Creative Writing

Student Name _____ Date _____

Knowledge of (check in box):   Poor   Adequate   Excellent

I.   Different Literary Genres

II.   Organization
      Unity, Clarity, Development

III   Mechanics
      Grammar, structure,
      spelling, punctuation

IV.   Style
      Creativity, emotional
      quality, imagination,
      theme, originality

V.   Understanding of Other
      Elements
      dialogue, special
      formal, setting,
      character development

VI.   Growth

Areas for future concentration:

Sample Evaluation Form #7

<u>Pupil Objective Self Report</u>

Student Name _____ Date _____

Please evaluate yourself by placing the letter a, b. or c on the line beside each item according to the scale below. Think of yourself in relation to your performance at the beginning of the independent study experience.

a - Diminishing   b - About the same   c - Increased

1. _____ Interest in school.
2. _____ Knowledge of topic being studied.
3. _____ Ability to make decisions.
4. _____ Ability to see relationships.
5. _____ Ability to solve problems.
6. _____ Knowledge of basic skills.
7. _____ Intellectual curiosity.
8. _____ Ability to formulate questions.
9. _____ Ability to work independently.
10. _____ Motivation toward learning.
11. _____ Status in peer group.
12. _____ Leadership ability.
13. _____ Ability to evaluate self.
14. _____ Research skills.

Sample Evaluation Form #8

Pupil Objective Self-Report

Student Name _____ Date _____

Rate yourself presently, in relation to your attitudes and abilities last year. Place the letters a, b, or c next to each item according to the following scale:

a – Diminishing   b – Increased   c – About the same

1. _____ I am more aware of my strengths and weaknesses.

2. _____ I am more willing to assume a leadership role.

3. _____ I have a greater interest in school.

4. _____ I am better able to make decisions.

5. _____ I am able to find information for myself.

6. _____ I am able to judge the usefulness of facts.

7. _____ I am able to see relationships.

8. _____ I am able to work independently.

9. _____ I am curious and want to learn about new things.

10. _____ I enjoy learning more.

11. _____ I am more willing to make things, experiment and use ideas.

12. Has the school year been helpful to you?

13. Has any part of the school year presented problems for you?

Sample Evaluation Form #9

Pupil Objective Self-Report

Student Name _____ Date _____

Use the following scale in responding to each of the items presented below. Place 1, 2, or 3 in the space provided.

       1 - independent study

       2 - regular class instruction

       3 - neither

1.   Which holds your interest more?   _____

2.   Which holds you more responsible for work?   _____

3.   In which do you express more creativity?   _____

4.   In which do teachers take more interest in you? _____

5.   In which do you put forth the greatest effort?   _____

6.   Which challenges you more?   _____

7.   Where do you believe you learn more?   _____

8.   Which improves your thinking?   _____

X.

Appendix

On the following pages are the appendices that have been previously referred to. They include:

#1 Student Interest Inventory
#2 Student Information from Parents
#3 Resource Development Questionnaire

These have been designed as examples and may be modified or redesigned to meet your instructional needs.

#4 Creative Problem Solving - An Example

This presents an actual example of how Creative Problem Solving (CPS) was integrated into an independent study that had real application value within the local community.

Appendix -1. Student Interest Inventory

NAME _____ DATE _____

1. What subjects do you like best in school? Number the following subjects from 1 to 8 in the order of your preference:

   _____ Reading   _____ Art   _____ Phys Ed

   _____ Music   _____ Science   _____ Other: _____

   _____ Social Studies   _____ Math   _____ _____

2. Are there any other subjects which you wish were a part of the school program? Name them:

3. What do you like to do when you come home from school?

4. Do you take any special classes? Name them:

5. Do you collect anything? What?

6. Do you like to read? What?

7. Name some of the books which you have enjoyed reading during the past year:

8. Do you read newspapers? Yes_____ No_____ If yes, which sections of the paper do you like best?

9. What have you done that you are most proud of?

10. Do you work best ...

    a. alone?

    b. with a friend?

    c. in a group?

11. Do you prefer to work ...

     a.   in a quiet area?   yes_____ no_____

     b.   with a moderate amount of noise?   yes_____ no_____

     c.   set apart from others?   yes_____ no_____

     d.   in a small group?   yes_____ no_____

     e.   in a large group?   yes_____ no_____

This inventory should be completed by the student and then discussed by student and teacher. Its purpose is to (1) assist student and teacher in focusing in on an area of interest which might provide the basis of an independent study and (2) find out how the student works best.

Appendix -2. Student Information from Parents

CHILD'S NAME_____   _____NAME___

Your child's hobbies or interests:

Projects which your child enjoys working on at home:

Interests when alone:

Interests with friends:

Interests with family members:

Books your child has enjoyed recently:

Unusual accomplishments, present or past:

Entered any competitions:

Special talents (music, art, athletics, etc.):

Private lessons:

Aspirations

Projects child enjoys doing:

Relationships with others:

Special needs:

Work and study habits:

General description of your child:

The purpose of this form is to provide additional information about the student to help find areas of interest for study.

Appendix -3. Resource Development Questionnaire

This form should be filled out by parents and community members. A resource file can be established for present and future use.

Name_____ Date_____

Occupation:

Hobby:

General interests:

Travel:

Vacations:

Special classes or training:

Past work experience:

Unusual experiences:

Contests or competitions:

Collections:

Appendix -4. Creative Problem Solving

The Creative Problem Solving method has been discussed in the Guide. This appendix describes the steps involved in the process of creative problem solving and illustrates its use through a sample study which was conducted by a group of gifted students. This study could have been done by an individual students just as well. Students coming across problems in their study can use this method.

Steps in Creative Problem Solving

Creative Problem Solving is a specific methodology for solving problems which fosters critical and productive thinking. If a student involved in independent study comes across a problem and wishes to seek solutions the following steps should be explained to the student in order to provide assistance.

The first stage of the process is called "The Mess". The problem as stated is not always the "real" problem and often consists of many sub-problems. Each step involves divergent thinking and convergent thinking. Students first brainstorm ideas for each step, then evaluate them before going on to the next step. The steps are as follows:

1. Fact Finding - In this step as much information as possible is gathered concerning the situation, e.g.:

    Who is involved?

    What is involved?

    Why is this a concern?

    When is this a concern?

    Where does this problem occur?

2. Problem Finding - The problem is redefined and stated in another way, e.g., How Might I _____? what is the real problem?

3. Idea Finding - Solutions for the problem are brainstormed. All ideas are listed, no matter how silly or impractical they appear.

4. Solution Finding - Evaluative criteria are established. These usually fall into areas such as cost, resources, space, time and attitudes. Solutions are listed on a grid. Criteria are placed at the top of the grid and values are assigned to each, i.e., on a scale of 1-4 with 1 being the best, how would you "judge" this idea?

5. Acceptance Finding - Who will help implement this idea? How will it best be implemented? Do I foresee any obstacles? Where should I begin? When?

Creative Problem Solving: An Example

An example of a study done by students using the previous steps follows:

The Mess: A group of sixth grade students became aware that litter was causing a problem in the community.

A.   Fact Finding

As part of the fact finding process, they decided to use surveys. They put together and distributed questionnaires. The results of the survey were analyzed so that they might:

1.   Create an awareness among residents that the problem exists.

2.   Find out the causes of the problem.

3.   Come up with solutions.

4.   Find other interested parties who might join in helping to solve the problem.

On the following pages are the questionnaires and the analyses of results.

Questionnaire -1.

LITTER QUESTIONNAIRE PLACED IN A LOCAL NEWSPAPER

<u>Community at Large</u>

1. Is litter a problem in the Community in the following areas?

    Residential   Schools & Fields   Vacant lots

    Shopping   Railroad Station   Other_____

2. Are there sufficient facilities to help dispose of litter?

3. What do you see as some of the causes of litter?

4. Do you have any suggestions as to how to help solve this problem?

5. Would you be willing to be a part of an anti-litter campaign?

Name_____ Address_____

ANALYSIS OF RESPONSES TO NEWSPAPER LITTER QUESTIONNAIRE

The responses received from placing the questionnaire in the newspaper were negligible. The students tried to list some of the reasons for this as follows:

1. Population apathetic

2. People are too lazy to fill out the form

3. People have too many other pressures and not enough time

4. Litter is not a problem

5. People receive the newspaper but don't read all parts of it.

In order to ascertain whether or not litter was a problem, they took the same survey and found that when they canvassed residents individually, residents did believe that litter was, indeed, a problem. The results of this follow-up survey are presented below:

1. Local collection of residential homes is not a problem.

2. The biggest problem appeared to be beer bottles and beer cans left on lawns and in parking lots.

3. Areas located near schools experience a greater amount of litter in streets and on their property.

Questionnaire -2.

LITTER QUESTIONNAIRE DISTRIBUTED TO

THE SIXTH-GRADE STUDENT POPULATION

To the 6th Grade Student Population

Please take a few moments and fill out the following questions:

1.   Are there areas in the school where you believe litter is a problem?
   _____

2.   What do you see as the causes?   _____

3.   Do you believe there are sufficient facilities to help dispose of litter in the schools?   _____

4.   Do you have any ideas as to how we might help eliminate litter in the schools? Please elaborate.   _____
   _____

5.   Would you be willing to participate in an anti-litter campaign?

Name _____   Class _____

ANALYSIS OF RESPONSES TO STUDENT LITTER QUESTIONNAIRE

The questionnaire was given to 6th grade students in both schools. The results were as follows:

1.   98% responded that litter was a problem in the schools.

2.   The cafeteria was the greatest problem.

3.   Most felt there were insufficient facilities for disposing of litter.

4.   67% agreed to be part of an anti-litter campaign.

Students realized that they could not solve all of the problems they would uncover this year but suggested the following solutions to school authorities:

1.   A student group be formed next year to follow through with information provided.

2.   Students be rewarded in some way for being involved.

3.   Explore possibility of adding facilities for disposal of litter especially in the cafeteria.

Questionnaire -3.

LITTER QUESTIONNAIRE DISTRIBUTED TO THE BOARD OF TRADE

We have been working with Dr. A. Gage of your organization to help solve the problem of litter in our community. We would very much appreciate it if you would take a few minutes to fill out the following questionnaire.

1.   How do you dispose of waste from your store or business?

2.   Do you feel you have sufficient facilities for disposal?

3.   What kinds of containers do you use?

4.   Are they open or closed?

5.   Do you have private or town services?

6.   Do you have any special problems in disposing of litter?

7.   Do others contribute to your problem? If so, how?

8.   Would you be willing to cooperate in an anti-litter campaign?

9.   Comments and suggestions.

Name_____   Address_____

ANALYSIS OF RESPONSES TO BOARD OF TRADE LITTER QUESTIONNAIRE

Of the 140 members of the Board of Trade, they received 7 responses. Storeowners responding did not have any major problems. Some did complain that residents left beverage containers in front of their sites. Some suggestions were:

1.   Additional litter baskets in community.

2.   More signs advising not to litter.

3.   Have store owners sweep litter from sidewalk into street for Sanitation Departments.

The students continued their fact finding and took a litter trip through the community so that they could establish areas in the school and streets that were a problem. They visited their local sanitation plant and met its manager. One of the Sanitation Commissioners came to their school and described the role of the Sanitation Department and the organizational ladder of how the Department fit into the Government. They learned that their local department was only responsible for collecting garbage from residents. The town was responsible for parking lots and empty fields, and store owners were responsible for their own areas.

The students played the simulation game "Democracy" so that they were able to learn more about how they might influence their legislators. They researched other materials to see what was already available on this subject. They visited a nearby community where a Citizens' Group had set up a successful recycling program in its community. They had overcome many obstacles and had a very successful operation.

The students decided to extend their efforts and include the entire 6th grade in what they were trying to do. The 6th grade teachers spoke with members of the Board of Trade and some of them agreed to sponsor a contest which would help to involve all sixth grade students and extend awareness that the problem existed:

The contest involved two parts:

Part I: Art - Design a Cover for our Litter Book

Part II: Ecology

The rules of the contest were:

1.   List as many items as possible that you throw away.

2.   Find a new use for them.

3.   If possible, make a model.

Winners would be judged on:

1.   Originality

2.   Cost

3.   Practicality

4.   Lasting Ability

B.   Problem Finding

The students redefined their problem. They decided to narrow down their problem even further. They defined their project in the following ways:

1.   Short Term Goal: How might we eliminate beer bottles and cans as a problem in our community?

2.   Long Term Goals: How might we eliminate the causes of litter in general? How might we eliminate the use of beer bottles and cans in our society?

C.   Idea Finding

The next step in the process involved idea finding. For this, they used the brainstorming method (See below).

They used their divergent thinking abilities. They did not evaluate or judge any of their ideas, but listed any and every idea that came to their minds. After they brainstormed their ideas, they used convergent thinking abilities and decided which ideas were best.

An example of how to use brainstorming to solve ecology problems would be to select an item which was usually thrown away, such as an egg carton and to list the many different ways it might be used.

Directions for Brainstorming

Brainstorming is a technique which is commonly used in group problem solving. There are some general guidelines which should be followed. The procedure is used to facilitate divergent or productive thinking.

1.   Critical judgment is ruled out. Criticism is often an idea-stopper or creativity killer. There should be a free flow of ideas.

2.   Unusual, wild or silly ideas are welcomed. Very often an idea that appears "crazy" will spark a wonderful idea. Group members will "piggy-back" on each other's ideas. Participants are encouraged to say anything that comes to mind, whether or not it appears related. The atmosphere created helps to stimulate the kind of thinking that produces unique and unusual ideas.

3.   Quantity is desirable - the more ideas the better. The greater the number of ideas, the greater the chance that some will be valuable.

4.   Combining and improving ideas is encouraged. After everyone's ideas have been recorded, review all of them to assess which ideas may be joined together and turned into better ideas.

The free play of imagination and fantasy establishes an atmosphere which sets the tone for creative, productive thinking.

DON'T THROW IT AWAY!

USE YOUR DIVERGENT THINKING ABILITIES

BRAINSTORM FOR FUN AND PLEASURE

HOW MANY WAYS CAN YOU USE AN EGG CARTON (Styroform)?

desk organizer
throw it
break it
recycle it
paint it
paint cups
drink from it
ice cube tray
use it for a bat
teething toy
make puppets
caterpillar
candy holder
outerspace animals
hovercraft
mini clocks
eyes for costumes
animal feeder
animal house
space ship
hold items such as nails
paint imprints

ears
top
mini car
magic tricks
collage
spice holder
coffin
rock collections
holiday decorations
flavored ices in freezer
plant plants
catch bugs with it
habit trail for hamster
dolls shoes
jump on it
golf ball holder
build things
beach toy
store clay
rock collector
tent for ants

POSSIBLE IDEAS FOR THE ELIMINATION OF BEER BOTTLES AND CANS

returnable beer bottles and cans
explodable containers
gold in bottle
win a prize if you return it
plastic bottles
recycling
magnets in buildings to attract and pile up litter
more garbage cans
inflatable beer bottles
different shapes that would seve as toys when empty
litter patrol
reusable glass
mirror on bottom
larger sizes
wax bottles
edible containers
larger fines for leaving them
contest for returning
rubber cans which bounce back at you
round and rubber - toy when finished
paper bottles
don't sell to any one under 25
pictures or autographs for collections
beer bottle is a lottery ticket
beer bottle becomes some kind of barter
buy one indestructible beer bottle which is refillable for life
picture of Ayatollah on garbage baskets for people to aim at
if you throw it in a basket, you win a prize
bottle becomes a musical instrument
bottle becomes a hat
bug beer bottle to track down owner
beer in solid form to be melted
if thrown on ground, you get a mild shock
readable bottles become a book
beer sold in gum form instead
chocolate containers
drop bottles on Iran
attach object which would not allow can or bottle to stay down when empty

D.   Solution Finding

As a result of their brainstorming, the students went on to solution finding and selected those ideas that they believed would be practical and which they could try to implement:

1. Returnable bottles

2. Giving a prize for returning bottles

3. Starting a recycling plant

4. Place more garbage disposal facilities in the community

5. Volunteer litter patrol

6. Paid litter patrol

7. Higher fines for littering

8. Raising the age to 25 for purchase of beer

9. Using only cans thereby eliminating bottles

The students also established criteria to evaluate these solutions:

1. Cost

2. Community acceptance

3. How much change would be involved

4. Will community residents become involved

5. Would community gain from it

6. Would government groups support it

7. Would it affect "big business"

8. Would it take away jobs

9. Would there be a cost to the taxpayer

10. Is it practical

11. Does it solve the problem

The students laid it out on a grid and assigned numbers from one (negative) to six (positive) to determine which of the nine ideas would be most suitable. Based on the research they had done, they came up with the following results:

	The Nine Ideas								
	1	2	3	4	5	6	7	8	9
Cost	2	3	6	4	6	3	3	6	4
Community Acceptance	3	5	5	4	6	3	2	2	2
Change	2	4	3	4	3	4	4	2	2
Resident Involvement	3	5	5	5	2	5	2	2	2
Community Gain	5	5	6	4	5	2	2	1	1
Government Support	1	3	5	3	4	3	2	2	1
Affect Big Business	1	2	6	6	6	6	6	2	1
Take Away Jobs	2	6	6	6	4	6	6	2	1
Cost to Taxpayer	2	2	6	2	6	1	3	3	6
Is it Practical	3	2	6	4	3	2	3	1	1
Solve Problem	4	4	5	3	6	6	1	1	1
TOTAL	28	41	59[1]	45	51[2]	41	34	22	

[1]Recycling Facility

[2]Volunteer Litter Patrol

80

E.   Acceptance Finding

The students proceeded to make recommendations, based on the results obtained from their evaluation and all of their research:

1.   Set up a recycling center.

2.   Some possible sites – Community Center
                           Parking Field behind T.S.S.
                           Store
                           Oceanside Sanitation Building

3.   Form an Advisory Board who would be responsible for setting up a Board of Directors.

4.   Board of Directors should include community members from all parts of our population, i.e., senior citizens, students (both from Project Extra and high school adolescent groups as well as other interested youth), community organizations, and government agencies.

5.   Litter patrol (volunteer force) be organized as a part of recycling group to include CETA workers and youth in our town who would get credit in schools for their involvement.

6.   Board should be responsible for reporting to County any problem areas.

7.   Senior citizen group would be ideal for daily supervision.

After the students completed their study they said they had gained the following insights:

a.   How to establish criteria in making decisions.

b.   That each cause has at least one effect.

c.   That there are many alternatives to solving problems.

d.   Different groups of people come up with different solutions to problems depending on their own interests.

e.   In establishing cost factors, demand makes prices go up.

f.   The price of one item may affect many others.

g.   How to use these ideas in our own lives when we do odd jobs to earn money.

h.   How to consider all factors involved when making decisions.

i.   How to list criteria with alternatives on a grid.

j.   How to consider social as well as economic factors when making decisions.

81

Bibliography

Altman, R. (1983). Social-emotional development of gifted children and adolescents: A research model. Roeper Review, 6(1), 65-68.

Bloom, B. (Ed.) (1956). Taxonomy of educational objectives: Cognitive domain. New York: David McKay.

Calkins, L.M. (1983). Lessons from a child. New Hampshire: Heinemann Educational Books.

Dirkes, M.A. (1983). Anxiety in the gifted: Pluses and minuses. Roeper Review, 6(1), 68-70.

Dressel, P.L., & Thompson, M.M. (1973). Independent study. San Francisco, CA: Jossey-Bass.

Guilford, J.P. (1977). Way beyond the I.Q.: A guide to improving intelligence and creativity. Buffalo, NY: Creative Education Foundation.

Isaacs, A.F. (1971). Biblical research IV: Perspectives on the problems of the gifted and possible solutions as revealed in the Pentateuch. The Gifted Child Quarterly, 15(1), 175-194.

Krueger, M.L. (1978). On being gifted. New York: Walker & Co.

Noller, R.B., Parnes, S., & Biondi, A. (1976). Creative actionbook. New York: Charles Scribners' Sons.

Parnes, S., Noller, R., & Biondi, A. (1977). Guide to creative action. New York: Charles Scribners' Sons.

Passow, A.H. (1981). The nature of giftedness and talent. The Gifted Child Quarterly, 25(1), 5-10.

Passow, A.H. (1982). Differentiated curricula for the gifted and talented. In S.N. Kaplan, P.H. Phenix, S.M. Reis, J.S. Renzulli, I.S. Sato, L.H. Smith, E.P. Torrance, & V.S. Ward (Eds.) Curricula for the gifted (pp. 4-25). Ventura, CA: Ventura County Superintendent of Schools Office.

Phenix, P.H. (1964). Realms of meaning. New York: McGraw-Hill.

Pressey, S.L. (1955). Concerning the nature of genius. The Scientific Monthly 81(3), 123-139.

Renzulli, J.S. (1975). A guidebook for evaluating programs for the gifted. Ventura, CA: Office of the Ventura County Superintendent of Schools.

Renzulli, J.S. (1982). What makes a problem real: Stacking the illusive meaning of qualitative differences in gifted education. The Gifted Child Quarterly, 26(4), 147-155.

Renzulli, J.S. (1983). Guiding the gifted in the pursuit of real problems: The transformed role of the teacher. The Journal for Creative Behavior, 17(1), 49-59.

Roeper, A. (1982). How the gifted cope with their emotions. Roeper Review, 5(2), 21-24.

Ross, A., & Parker, M. (1980). Academic and social self-concepts of the academically gifted. Exceptional Children, 37(2), 6-10.

Tannenbaum, A.J. (1983). Gifted children: Psychological and educational perspectives. New York: Macmillan.

Terman, L.M., & Oden, M.H. (1947). The gifted child grows up, (Vol. IV). Stanford, CA: Stanford University Press.

Terrassier, J. (1979). Gifted children and psychopathology: The syndrome of dyssynchrony. In J.J. Gallagher (Ed.), Gifted Children: Reaching their potential (pp. 434-440). Jerusalem, Israel: Kollek & Sons, Ltd.

Tippecanoe School Corporation. (1980). PACE. Lafayette, Indiana: Author.

Treffinger, D.J. (1975). Teaching for self-directed learning: A priority for the gifted and talented. The Gifted Child Quarterly, XIX(1), 46-59.

Whitmore, J.R. (1980). Giftedness, conflict and under-achievement. Boston, MA: Allyn & Bacon.

Wolf, R.M. (1979). Evaluation in education: Foundations of competency assessment and program review. New York: Praeger Publications.

Student Resource Book

The "Independent Learner" Student Resource Book is an integral component of the independent study program as set forth in this book. It is published separately so that each student may have a concise reference to use as a guide in implementing and assimilating the independent study process when working alone.

Both the Teacher's Manual and the Student Resource Book have been field tested in a variety of settings including pull out programs for the gifted, homogemeous classes for the gifted and in the regular classroom.

A number of teachers gave each one of their students a copy of the Resource Book and used independent study with the entire class. Other teachers selected a group of students for independent study and gave each a Resource Book. Some teachers took a skills approach to the Resource Book activities and taught them to the entire class. They then distributed copies of the Resource Book to the students to use in an independent study.

Teachers are encouraged to use the material in ways that are appropriate to their own setting. The Manual and Resource Book have been designed so that independent study can be an option in every classroom.